BUILDING CIVILIAN-MILITARY COLLABORATION TO ENHANCE RESPONSE FOLLOWING AN ANTHRAX RELEASE

Background

A deliberate release of aerosolized anthrax could be catastrophic to a community's medical, financial and civil infrastructure, and could also result in a loss of trust in the government.[1,2] Comprehensive planning is conducted by local, state and federal health and homeland security departments to anticipate these problems and to develop functional response plans for, among other activities, the distribution of medical countermeasures to prevent illness and death. Fundamental questions and confusion persist in the civilian community regarding the potential military contributions of personnel and resources in the case of a deliberate release of anthrax. A focused literature review was unsuccessful in providing evidence of this civilian knowledge deficit of military capabilities and willingness to support community efforts.

Many civilian preparedness planners are not aware of the capabilities, resources and regulations guiding the Department of Defense's (DoD) ability to augment local governments in the case of a catastrophic event. Defense Support of Civil Authorities (DSCA) is, in fact, an important military mission. [3,4] DoD has a variety of personnel, materiel, and equipment readily available to deploy throughout the nation as circumstances overwhelm local and state resources. Pre-event knowledge of DoD efforts and potential capabilities to provide local assistance will aid the strategic development of all-hazards disasters plans, including the dispensing of medical countermeasures (MCM).

The purpose of this paper is to provide basic information to civilian health and emergency response agencies regarding potential local, National Guard and federal DoD resources available in the event of a deliberate release of aerosolized anthrax. Additionally, this paper will suggest steps that can be taken to develop collaborative civilian-military relationships and coalitions. By enhancing these alliances, the response to a catastrophic event, including the timely and sustainable dispensing of medical countermeasures, can be improved and the preparedness of the Nation strengthened.[5]

Anthrax – an enduring threat!

The deliberate release of aerosolized Anthrax remains a threat to national health security.[6] The Center for Disease Control (CDC) prioritizes anthrax as a Category 1 Agent due to its characteristics that include: ease of dissemination, high mortality, potential to cause social disruption, and the extensive planning and preparation necessary to achieve readiness.[7,8] Exposure to aerosolized *Bacillus anthracis* requires rapid delivery and administration of ciprofloxacin or doxycycline prophylaxis within 48 hours of the decision to treat.[9] The planning guidance includes dispensing an initial 10-day supply of antibiotics followed by fifty additional dosing days for a complete course of 60 day treatments to achieve maximum efficacy. Post exposure treatment profiles are more complex for certain populations, such as pregnant women.[10]

In addition to a course of antibiotic therapy, post exposure vaccine is recommended to sterilize spores and mitigate latent disease. Post exposure vaccination with Anthrax Vaccine Adsorbed (AVA) is administered subcutaneously three times over a month (0, 2, and 4 weeks) in addition to 60 days of antibiotic protection for optimal outcomes.[10]

The determination of length and type of antibiotic prophylaxis and the use of post-exposure vaccine places large workforce, materiel and logistical burdens on the civilian public health sector. Although local and state preparedness planners have put forth deliberate efforts to develop and implement strategies that ensure adequate MCM distribution and dispensing, concerns remain regarding the public health sector's ability to meet this requirement due to limited (and shrinking) personnel, competing priorities, and diminishing budgets.[11,12,13]

Expanding Civilian Capabilities to Address Anthrax Attacks

<u>Federal Mandates</u>

In the past ten years there have been increasing expectations placed upon the public health sector regarding preparedness.[14]   Many federally funded programs have been initiated to augment and guide state and local authorities in program development and mission assistance at every level of government.[15]

In 2004, The Cities Readiness Initiative (CRI) established federal funding for select large cities to focus on preparedness response to bioterror incidence.[16]   CRI now encompasses 72 metropolitan areas, covering over 57% of the U.S. citizenry and all fifty states. Budgetary constraints now place over 70 percent of the CRI cities at risk from program elimination. The infusion of federal funds and grants to state and local public health departments allowed cities to build infrastructure, hire personnel and expand training, but also broadened the public health mission to emergency preparedness planning including bioterror contingencies such as MCM dispensing processes.[17]

In December 2006, the Pandemic and All-Hazards Preparedness Act (PAHPA) changed the mission focus of public health in many ways.[18]   For example, the Hospital Preparedness Program, coordinated through the state health departments, calls for establishing community response teams including hospitals, fire departments and public health agencies and coordinating plans and capabilities for significant health incidents.[19]

Recognizing the importance of timely medical countermeasure dispensing, in December 2009, Presidential Executive Order (EO) 13527 (Establishing Federal Capabilities for the Timely Provision of Medical Countermeasures Following a Biological Attack) was signed. [20]   The intent of this Executive Order was captured in the newly developed Federal Interagency Concept of Operations Plan for dispensing MCM (FICOP-MCM). This comprehensive guidance articulated the roles and responsibilities of federal agencies including: Department of Homeland Security (DHS), the Department of Health and Human Services (HHS), the Veterans Administration, DoD, and the Federal Emergency Management Agency (FEMA) for MCM distribution following a biologic attack with respect to a coordinated effort in the first 48 hours after the decision to dispense MCMs.[9]

New Public Health Responsibilities

The new requirements set forth to prepare the nation for the increased biological threat caused a competition for resources in the public health community. The broad specialty of CBRN preparedness and planning was not an area historically assigned to public health. There was vast amount of knowledge to gain, in addition to maintaining the "traditional" public health mission of disease prevention and community health promotion. Augmenting skill sets required for chemical, biological, radiological and nuclear (CBRN) threats as well as preparedness for pandemics caused a strain on budgets. Although "new" federal funding helped support the initial years of the public health biodefense effort, there was a lingering cost borne by other non-biodefense and preparedness programs. For example, childhood immunizations and tuberculosis prevention programs suffered in some locations.[14,21] Fifty-seven percent of local public health departments nationwide have reported eliminating or reducing a major operational program in 2011.[22] Reductions in preventive services will compound the preparedness challenge by potentially increasing the size of medically vulnerable populations, such as the obese and smokers, and those with chronic health conditions.

Public heath funding decreased in 40 states over the past year and difficult decisions must be made as to which local programs or services will remain funded.[23] In late 2011, both the House and Senate approved PAHPA reauthorization to continue the funding necessary to sustain critical preparedness initiatives.[24] Potential federal budgets cuts to programs such as the HHP and CRI will impact local and state departments required to cover the deficits. Since 2005, federal funds for state and local preparedness have already decreased by 38 percent. The Assistant Secretary for Preparedness and Response, RADM Nichole Lurie, testified to the Senate Committee on Homeland Security and Government Affairs that "without continued support and funding for our public health and medical system, the infrastructure could begin to degrade and health outcomes may be affected."[11]

Preparing for an anthrax attack is only one of countless CBRN scenarios for which a community must prepare.[25] Just as each locality has their unique weather and natural disasters to anticipate such as earthquakes, wild fires and hurricanes, emergency preparedness resources need to be prioritized based on the community's perceived threats. All- Hazards Planning does consolidate the efforts for some generalized aspects of planning such as coordinating the volunteer resources and assigning specific locations for alternate care facilities. However, every specific biologic threat has its own medical intervention with varying timelines for effective implementation of the intervention, often requiring expert knowledge in the sub-specialty. Many threats require vast amounts of planning, agility, and extensive resources. Emergency preparedness (which was reduced or eliminated in 23 percent of local public health departments surveyed recently) is just a part of the public health mission that ranges from smoking cessation to pregnancy prevention.[12,22] These competing missions stress the limited assets of communities.

Additionally, the biodefense mission required new relationships with law enforcement officers, health care and private sector medical providers, and hospitals. These coalition relationships, originally established for preparedness functions, translated to joint population health missions such as education of community groups and preventive medicine opportunities. The public health community expanded its area of influence through information sharing. Working in partnership with community leaders and diverse organizations, they contacted groups they had not previously interacted with, and collaborated with them.[26]

Planning for disaster requires comparing threats presented with available capabilities. In some respects, the preparedness effort was biased towards urban areas due to the vulnerabilities associated with high value targets and dense populations. Many types of plans evolved to address the spectrum of socio-economic and demographic diversity across US communities. There are potentially thousands of different MCM distribution plans created by all levels of government; one prescribed plan will not work for all cities or regions, because of unique regional characteristics, such as varying medical resources and different community expectations of government assistance in disasters. However, the harmonization of plans across government and the private sector within a region is essential.

Only the local community can accurately assess the most appropriate MCM distribution plan for their unique location. There is some thought that rural communities are not considered "high risk" for the anthrax scenario as their widely dispersed population may not be a likely a terrorist target.[27] The community planners' perception of risk will impact the time and effort a rural community places towards planning for these types of scenarios. The diversity of urban and rural populations and their differing healthcare systems and infrastructures present complexities when coordinating medical and logistic efforts for disaster planning. For example, transportation is vastly different in a small farm county where privately owned diesel trucks may be the primary mode of transportation for individual families when compared to the issues for a family reliant on bus or subway transportation in a city. Availability of primary care providers, local pharmacies, and number of volunteers all impact the appropriate type of dispensing model for a given location. Additionally, some rural communities did not benefit from the additional CRI funding that enhanced other programs surrounding "preparedness".[13] Many isolated counties already lag behind in acquiring advances such as equipment for detecting and containing hazardous material and advanced training for disaster responders.[14]

The distribution of public health personnel also impacts the local community preparedness planning. With over 2,800 public health departments nation-wide, each of these have varying levels of preparedness and response expertise.[28] Two-thirds of the local public health agencies provide services to areas with populations of less than 50,000 people possibly leaving populations underserved.[29] Substantial shortages of public health professionals and nurses exist compounded by national vacancy rates, for public health positions, varying from eleven to thirty percent.[12,29,30] Between 2008 and 2010, over 46,000 state and local public health jobs were lost and 23 percent of the public health workforce are currently eligible to retire.[5] The current staffing challenges may be insurmountable in the wake of a catastrophic event requiring augmentation of their staffing plans. Further burdens are now placed on public health entities as the majority of the states continue to decrease local funding.[23]

The Challenges Continues...

After ten years of increased funding and federal guidance, there is still plenty of room for regional and national improvement: time to develop disaster preparedness and CBRN expertise; expand local emergency management; and continue to foster collaborative relationships among regional, state and federal agencies. Two major 2011 reports highlighted some challenges facing the public health efforts. One gave the nation a grade of "D" for the ability to dispense MCMs after a large-scale event.[31] The other warned of the potential detrimental implications a weak economy could have on preparedness advances made over the past decade.[23]

Persistent public health sector response gaps can be mitigated with resource sharing and by building coalitions using a "whole of community" approach.[32] Local military installations should be considered one of those resources.[33] The Department of Health and Human Services' National Health Security Strategy states that all levels of government should support a community's health to "protect them from and support them during an incident."[5(pg.2)] Some civilian preparedness planners and leaders are not aware of DoD resources or how to begin the communication process to establish these mutually beneficial relationships. Once initial contact is established, both the local community and the DoD installation can provide their unique expertise to enhance the safety and security of their shared population.

Department of Defense Capabilities

The Chief of Staff of the Army often speaks of "maintaining the trust with the American people".[34] With military engagements potentially decreasing after ten years of active conflict in the Global War on Terrorism in Iraq and Afghanistan, and the armed services restructured reduction in force, it is imperative to maintain America's trust and high confidence.[35] The Nation needs assurance that even as the defense budget decreases;

7

the military will continue to safeguard key security interests. Working with local community planners serves the dual purpose of maintaining this trust and providing national security.

<u>The DSCA Mission</u>

In February 2012, President Obama, supported by Secretary of Defense Leon Panetta, the Chairman of the Joint Chiefs of Staff GEN Martin Dempsey, and the Chiefs of Staff of each of the military branches presented the new National Strategic Plan at the Pentagon. The strategy states the Military will continue to protect the homeland and provide defense support to civilian authorities (DSCA) in two of the ten primary missions:[3]

> ***Defend the Homeland and Provide Support to Civil Authorities***. *U.S. forces will continue to defend U.S. territory from direct attack by state and non-state actors. We will also come to the assistance of domestic civil authorities in the event such defense fails or in case of natural disasters, potentially in response to a very significant or even catastrophic event.*

> ***Conduct Humanitarian, Disaster Relief, and Other Operations.*** *The nation has frequently called upon its Armed Forces to respond to a range of situations that threaten the safety and well-being of its citizens and those of other countries. U.S. forces possess rapidly deployable capabilities, including airlift and sealift, surveillance, medical evacuation and care, and communications that can be invaluable in supplementing lead relief agencies, by extending aid to victims of natural or man-made disasters, both at home and abroad. DoD will continue to develop joint doctrine and military response options to prevent and, if necessary, respond to mass atrocities.*

The 2010 Quadrennial Defense Review (QDR), a military strategic roadmap issued every four years to guide near and long term planning, focused consequence management organizations to field faster, more flexible lifesaving capabilities and reduce response times in support of domestic CBRN incidents.[36] DoD's posture continues as an augmentation force; assisting state and local governments with extensive military resources, including personnel, to distribute MCMs if requested. Citizens expect the military to assist in times of disaster, either natural or man-made.[37] "It's powerful just to see National Guard vehicles driving by. It gives people the sense that they're not by themselves and that help is coming," Honorable W. Craig Fugate, FEMA Administrator.[38]

DoD will respond to DSCA missions but regulatory statutes and organizational systems can be confusing and complicated for non-DoD agencies to understand. Two key guiding documents for military support to civilians include the Department of Defense Directive (DoDD) 3025.18, "Defense Support of Civil Authorities (DSCA)" (2010) and Department of Defense Instruction (DoDI) 6200.03 "Public Health Emergency Management Within the Department of Defense" (2010). As a result of thorough analysis and external recommendation, DoD has modified the leadership cell, structure and type of units assigned, and deployment time frame of the Defense CBRN Response Enterprise to meet changing requirements.[39,40,41] These reorganizations and realignments of DoD units will result in optimized command and control to decrease duplication of effort, ensure the appropriate response force is activated, and improve response times.

It is important to remember that DoD is almost always a support service, which means that its role is to provide limited local, and specific services with the intent of "last in and first out" once the local and state governments can resume handling the situation.[42] It is not the intent of a DoD unit to assume responsibility for an over-all mission: the goal is to augment the local and state governments with the personnel, supplies and equipment they request at their location.

Federal and National Guard Overview

The DoD response to support civilian authorities includes the joint service members of the Army, Navy, Air Force and Marines. In addition to federal forces, each state has their own National Guard force dedicated to the protection and welfare of its state's citizens. The National Guard can also be federalized. Federal military forces (active duty and reserve component) and National Guard are regulated by different laws and policies.[1] In a state led response to emergencies, state governors have authority over their National Guard and mobilize and utilize this resource expeditiously. Federal forces are activated after the Secretary of Health and Human Services declares a public health emergency, or if a governor requests federal assistance from the President who declares an emergency under the Stafford Act and a validated request for assistance is received.[43, 44] DoD does not have the authority to respond without a request.

Delayed military activation for Hurricane Katrina led to improvements in the current command and control structure for DoD forces to expedite the federal response.[38] Active duty units were prepositioned to assist with supplies and transportation assets prior to the hurricane making landfall, but these essential services were delayed as the legal aspects of mobilization were verified.[45] During Katrina, the military liaison position between the preparedness community and the active duty military was just one of many missions assigned to an officer to coordinate. The Army now permanently assigns a Defense Coordinating Officer (DCO) to each of the ten FEMA regional headquarters to serve as the Secretary of Defense's primary contact.[46] This active duty colonel and his staff aid the collaborative effort from the joint field office that also houses the Federal Coordinating teams and interfaces with the State coordinating team, to ensure that all federal resources are expeditiously deployed when requested.[47]

"Dual Status Command" was recently established to unify the federal and National Guard command structure. Previously each had "parallel" command and independently led their own units, which resulted in duplication of services and poor communication. Now, once a large-scale military effort is requested, command and control falls under U.S. Northern Command with a general officer providing the instrumental oversight of all

---

[1] National Guard forces can be activated in one of three ways: as a State funded force, under control of the Governor- Title 32, as a federally funded state force, under control of the governor – Title 32, or as a federally funded force- Title 10, under federal control and then under the restrictions of Posse Comitatus as other "federal DoD military"

military resources.[48]   The Commander of Northern Command stated this is the most important DCSA initiative in a decade.[49]

The evolving role of the DCO and Dual Status Commander for the joint DoD forces decreased the duplication of services and improved unity of effort. The modified CBRN Enterprise was transformed to restructure the smaller state controlled response teams to be augmented by the larger multi-service national response force that now responds more quickly with a more diverse of range of capabilities.

Understanding the Organizational Structure and Resources of DoD
Established in October 2002 to coordinate the DoD homeland defense missions after the increased threats of 9/11, U.S. Northern Command (NORTHCOM) is the military combatant command responsible for planning, organizing, and executing all aspects of homeland defense and DSCA missions (U.S. Pacific Command provides this mission for Hawaii and the territories in the pacific).   Under NORTHCOM, U.S. Army North (ARNORTH) is charged as the dedicated joint land force component of homeland defense. Joint Task Force- Civil Support (JTF-CS), a subordinate of ARNORTH, plans and integrates DoD domestic CBRN consequence management support.[50] Understanding the organization's structure helps to clarify the process in which missions are approved and assigned.

Table 1 – Organizational Structure - see appendix A

Joint Task Force-Civil Support (JTF-CS)'s mission is to provide quickly deployable forces to support operations intended to save lives, prevent further injury, and enable community recovery primarily in response to a CBRN incident.[51]   JTF-CS provides command and control to the federal CBRN units consisting of aviation, logistics, medical, and operations units and assets. The scope of the emergency must exceed the capabilities of local and state resources before federal assistance is provided. Under

11

the regulatory guidance prohibiting Posse Comitatus, federal forces can provide civil support, but cannot be directly involved with law enforcement activities.[2,42]

DoD CBRN Enterprise

Federal Resources

The Defense CBRN Response Force (DCRF) consists of Task Forces: Aviation, Logistics, Medical, and Operations. Primary capabilities include urban search and rescue, patient decontamination, casualty ground/air evacuation, and general logistical support.[51] Composed of 5200 Soldiers, Sailors, Airmen, and Marines, almost half arrive within 24 hours of activation. Yearlong unit rotations include training and exercises to expand proficiency in CBRN and civil support missions. The QDR required DoD to change the focus of the DCRF to expedite arrival in order to assist with MCM distribution.[36] The federal Command and Control (C2) CBRN Element (C2CRE) can augment capabilities including medical, search and rescue, engineering, and transportation. These national resources are flexible and modified to meet requirements based on the type and size of the incident.

The specific units that have the appropriate skill sets consistent with a request are activated. For example, if the local community needs trucks and communications equipment, the appropriate teams are deployed to effectively meet the requirement without overwhelming the system. If the situation changes, the C2 element can coordinate additional personnel and assets to the scale needed.

National Guard Resources

The National Guard's unique mission is providing rapid response and assistance in its home state with over 3140 armories and air guard stations nationally.[52] For example, when disastrous tornados struck the Midwest in March 2012 killing 40 citizens and causing an estimated two billion dollars in damage, the National Guard arrived within

---

[2] Posse Comitatus allows Federal forces (active duty and reserve forces) to provide defense support to civil authorities (DSCA) but they cannot be directly involved with law enforcement activities. They can secure federal property and protect government supplies. The National Guard forces, when controlled by the governor under Title 10, do not fall under the jurisdiction of Posse Comitatus.

hours, providing medical assistance as they aided with the search and rescue mission.[53,54,55] In 2011 alone, the National Guard volunteered over 907,180 duty days in support of disaster relief.[56] In a CBRN event, the National Guard would be the first DoD responders to augment civilian capabilities with their unique teams and logistic packages.

The National Guard aligns its ten Homeland Response Forces (HRFs) in the states where the FEMA regional headquarters are located to provide strong ties to federal and state resources.[57] The 566 person teams deploy on 6-12 hour notice with a robust C2 element, search and extraction teams, decontamination capability, and medical assets.[58] There are 57 Weapon of Mass Destruction – Civil Support Teams (WMD-CSTs) deployable within two hours to provide assistance and facilitate additional DoD units.[59] CBRN Enhanced Response Force Packages (CERFP) include 17 units of 186 personnel structured for search and extraction, decontamination, emergency medical triage and treatment and C2 prepared to activate within six hours.

Table 2 – CBRN Enterprise - see Appendix A

DoD Organization at the Local Level

Just as each civilian community is unique, every DoD installation is different. They vary by the branch that runs the military location; the major function of the activity (training, infantry, naval, etc.); and even the level of medical services (medical center, community hospital, clinic). This desired flexibility and capability, however, also impedes offering a "standard approach" to the civilian sector when military assets are requested. There are some helpful consistencies; many basic tenant organizations remain constant throughout all DoD installations and key leaders are assigned at every military installation to facilitate civil-military relations and provide support in time of disaster.

During the first moments after an incident, all response is local. Only a military installation located nearby would be readily available to assist civilian entities due to the length of time required to deploy forces from other locations. DoD leadership intends that local military commanders anticipate helping their community, such as, develop Memoranda of Understandings (MOUs) to address known gaps in capabilities and resources.[43] Military medical treatment facilities (MTFs), military police and fire departments frequently have mutual aid agreements with the local community departments and have long-established coalitions.[60] Most MTFs are involved in training exercises with the local public health department and emergency response governing bodies as required by national hospital accreditation agencies.[61, 62] These MOUs and mutual aid agreements are based on the availability of military assets but establish commitments between civilian and military authorities to build lasting coalitions.

Military establishments increase security measures in the event of a suspected bioterror incident. The military must sustain mission-critical operations and essential services but will "coordinate and collaborate to the maximum extent possible" with civilian counterparts.[58]

In the case of a deliberate release of anthrax, as an example, the local military installation could possibly assist the community in ways that include providing equipment, transportation, and personnel. Generators, light sets and refrigeration equipment may be needed at the incident site or community level Points of Distribution (PODs) for the dispensing of medical countermeasures. Military buses, ambulances and air assets (either helicopters or airplanes) may be required to assist with moving supplies or evacuating the ill, injured or displaced citizens. Additional manpower, both medical and non-medical, is often required in times of disaster. Prior coordination will expedite the request for these assets, if they are available.

As an important related issue, DoD regulates that MCM distribution to active duty service members is conducted only via closed PODs.[58] Distribution plans for the family members of active duty service members and the military retiree population are flexible and at the discretion for each installation. Many military communities have large retiree populations. If the local base or post provided MCMs for all their beneficiaries and personnel on the installation, it could significantly reduce the demand for public health

14

services in a public health emergency. Working together, the local military and civilian community could develop MCM distribution plans to feasibly cover the entire population while building mutually beneficial agreements to address gaps in resources should an event occur.

Facilitating working relationships with a military post or base begins with an understanding of the key leaders involved with the decision making process for emergency response. During a disaster, the city or county officials would coordinate with the local installation commander's staff. The Installation Commander is responsible for the safety and welfare of the entire population of the post. The Hospital Commander is responsible for the health of the extended military community as the installation Director of Health Services.[63] The MTF Emergency Manager is responsible for planning the preparedness and operational execution of all-hazards emergency management activities for the Hospital Commander.[58] The Public Health Emergency Officer is a clinician who provides the commander with critical guidance and recommendations to respond to public health emergencies. These military leaders are only a few of the influential personnel who advise the base or post commander during emergencies.

Local installation commanders maintain "Immediate Response Authority" to authorize service members to augment local communities in emergency situations in "order to save lives, prevent human suffering, or mitigate great property damage" if requested from local authorities.[4] Requests by local government to the local military command can expedite assistance, temporarily, in less than 24 hours.[58] This gives state governors time to formally request federal assistance. Establishing strong working relationships and collaborative agreements to support each other set the foundation needed when disaster strikes.

Table 3 – Key Personnel- see Appendix A

Building Civilian-Military Collaboration

Many civilian-military communities have developed strong relationships and enduring coalitions. Recently, when one Division Surgeon was asked how his local community would ask for help from the military installation, he said, "The Mayor would just call the Commander."[64] This statement is indicative of many communities' who have built embedded relationships with "their" post. Other civilians have difficulty knowing how to interact with the military. Based on prior experiences, some may be intimidated by the structure or not realize the depth of defense assistance to civil authorities in disasters and the importance of this DoD mission.[65] DoD needs to provide education to the civilian community regarding the range of essential support services the military can provide during times of domestic need.

Examples of Best practice between DoD and Civilian Communities

Many examples of best practices exist throughout the country. For years, the South Potomac Civilian-Military Community Relations Council (COMREL) has joined the leadership of two naval bases, the town and multi-county governments to discuss a range of issues forging partnerships across their communities.[66] One of the cooperative efforts noted by COMREL was the comprehensive emergency services in the area, which noted that the "longstanding mutual aid agreements" among the civilian and military communities better prepare all for a crisis.[67] A more focused partnership is the Seattle Urban Area Security Initiative (UASI) whose mission is to ensure military and federal agencies develop a regional recovery framework dealing with the ramifications of a catastrophic anthrax attack.[68] The group has used workshops, tabletop exercises and interviews with all levels of local, state, federal, military and private participants to devise a plan realizing increased coordination and collaboration across agencies.

Walter Reed Army Medical Center and the National Disaster Medical System hospitals of Maryland overcame 20 years of a lack of civilian-military training exercises of critical services.[69] By participating in tabletop and functional exercises, there is now a strong, workable mutual aid agreement to ensure the appropriate surge capacity for overseas mass casualties.

A proven example of collaborative community effort was the swift response and coordinated effort provided in Central Texas following the shooting incident at Fort Hood in November 2009.[70] The result of years of integrated planning, coordination, and exercises between the post and the surrounding communities greatly enhanced the response and mutual aid assistance saving lives. Eighteen years earlier, Fort Hood had provided emergency care and treatment in a similar tragedy when a shooter killed 23 and wounded another 20 victims at the Luby's Restaurant in Killeen, TX.[71] Now this joint community works together daily to function well in extreme situations. "Organizations that routinely collaborate with others and encourage and foster such activities are likely to be more successful at coordination than those that do not."[72]

Successive Steps to Follow

The first step towards building collaboration is identifying good points of contact. In most cases, this should begin with the Installation Commander. He or she is accountable for the health and welfare of all service members assigned to the Installation under his/her command. From there introductions will be facilitated to other key leaders as mentioned earlier in this paper. For communities not located near a military base, coordinating a meeting with the Defense Coordinating officer at the FEMA Regional headquarter provides a starting point that leads to facilitated meetings with both active duty and National Guard resources. Once the key leaders have met, the next step in the partnership building is to establish a mutually beneficial "joint council".

Many civilian-military community joint councils start as larger entities aimed at information sharing or social groups with business leaders. In 2000, Pittsburgh communities formed an alliance with the region's DoD resources to emphasize the economic and quality of life effects the local military provided to the 10 counties of western Pennsylvania.[73] The group further focused on coordinating resources for emergency management and included a cooperative response, uniquely tying in military, civilian, public and private partners. As Joint councils are developed, the needs of the community can be assessed and then specific work groups can focus on gaps in resources and plans developed to address the short falls.

Military Medical Treatment Facilities (MTFs), military police and fire departments typically have had long standing mutual aid agreements with their civilian counter parts and well-established working relationships. Ensuring public health departments are involved in the planning process of all aspects of emergency and disaster planning is essential and often overlooked. DoD leadership instructs local military commanders to develop Memoranda of Understandings (MOUs) that address known gaps in resources.[43] Establishing the civilian–military community commitment on paper needs to be tested and verified with realistic exercises.

Each level and type of exercise serves a purpose, all of which lead to enhanced response. The goal of the exercise needs to be clear for all participants. Many exercises are required to meet state or federal requirements for a specific department. Coordination of exercises should be mutually beneficial for all involved to increase participation and decrease cost. Large scale exercises build alliances with local, state and federal partners. The "Vibrant Response" exercises are national military exercises scheduled numerous times a year to test the limits of responder's knowledge and resources involving a dual scenario, such as including a weather disaster with a CBRN incident. One of the challenges with the large scale federal exercises is the requirement that local and state resources must be "overwhelmed" in the scenario so that federal forces can participate. All levels of leadership and responders need to participate to simulate a true event. [74,75, 76] An Arizona exercise included more than 250 agencies and 8,000 emergency personnel; including National Guard Soldiers from six states. The dual scenarios of a catastrophic flood and the detonation of a ten-kiloton Improvised Nuclear Device in the Phoenix metropolitan area provided local, state and federal agencies diverse experiences to assess their performance.[77] Exercises like these provide federal, state and local partners important opportunities to work together to ensure future joint mission success. Exercise evaluation is essential, both informally as the training is conducted and in a written after-action report once the exercise is completed. This helps ensure that lessons learned are documented and will contribute to modifications and improvement in the action plan.[78]

Conclusion

Protecting the Homeland and Defense Support of Civilian Authorities have been long-standing missions for the military and will remain a priority. DoD is uniquely capable of augmenting local and state entities in the case of a bioterror event. As local public health departments face the challenges of multiple competing missions and decreasing federal and state funding, they will have to turn to coalition building to augment services and resources, especially in time of disaster. Local DoD installation leadership and personnel are prepared to support the communities in which they are located. Building partnerships and coalitions, forging joint councils, developing mutual aid agreements and MOAs, and providing realistic training exercises will prepare these civilian-military communities to respond to disasters together to decrease the morbidity and mortality from a catastrophic event. The unique challenges of CBRN response, including the timely distribution of medical countermeasures in the event of a deliberate anthrax release, have been addressed by the federal CBRN Response Enterprise. These federal and National Guard units are prepared to rapidly deploy as requested when local and state resources are overwhelmed. Collaborative agreements and synchronizations must continue at local, state and federal level to optimize emergency response plans with regards to CBRN incidents.

DoD capabilities can provide key manpower augmentation, logistical support, and subject matter expertise especially with bioterror preparedness planning and distribution of MCMs in the event of a deliberate anthrax release. Mitigation can result from early assistance from DoD partners at all levels in a truly whole of nation effort. DoD is committed to providing DSCA to save lives and decrease the pain and suffering of American citizens in the case of a catastrophic event. DoD's support to civilian authorities and the ongoing cooperation at the local, state, and federal levels will: improve disaster response plans, bolster homeland defense, support vital national security interests, and increase the publics' trust and confidence in our government, military, and public health agencies.

APPENDIX A

Table 1 – Organizational Structure

COMMAND	MISSION	HIGHER HEADQUARTERS	LOCATION
U.S. Northern Command **NORTHCOM**	-Partners to conduct homeland defense, civil support and security cooperation to defend and secure the United States and its interests	Secretary of Defense	Peterson Air Force Base, Colorado Springs, CO
U.S. Army North **ARNORTH**	-Execute DoD's homeland defense and civil support operations in the land domain -Further develop, organize and integrate DoD CBRNE response capabilities and operations -Build the capability to perform the Joint Force Land Component Command and the Army Service Component Command functions -Secure land approaches to the homeland	NORTHCOM	Fort Sam Houston, San Antonio, TX
Joint Task Force-Civil Support **JTF-CS**	-The federal *operational* standing joint task force headquarters for chemical, biological, radiological, and nuclear (CBRN) response operations - Anticipates, plans, and prepares for CBRN response operations -Deploys to command and control DOD forces and conducts CBRN response operations in support of civil authorities in order to save lives, prevent further injury, and provide temporary critical support to enable community recovery	ARNORTH	Fort Eustis, Newport News, VA

42, 51,79

Table 2 – CBRN Enterprise

UNIT	Number Of Units	Personnel Assigned	Force assigned	Response Time	Assignment	CAPIBILITIES
Defense CBRNE Response Force **DCRF**	1	5200	Federal -active duty	2100-24 hours 3100- 48 hours	AD Units assigned for a one year rotation	Aviation, medical, logistics, and command and control (C2)
Command and Control CBRN Response Elements **C2CRE**	2	1500	Federal -active duty and reserve component	92 hours		Assessment, search and extraction, casualty decontamination, emergency medical, Level II medical, security, engineering, C2, logistics, transportation
CBRNE Enhanced Response Force Packages **CERFPs**	17	186	National Guard -25% full time duty	6-12 Hours	States	Search & extraction, decontamination, emergency triage and treatment, C2
Homeland Response Force **HRF**	10	566	National Guard -25% full time duty	6-12 HOURS	By states in each of the 10 FEMA regions	All CERFP capabilities expanded for a larger mission and 200 man security attachment with increased C2
Weapons of Mass Destruction Civil Support Teams **WMD-CST**	57	22	National Guard -full time duty	Initial elements: 1.5 hours Main body: 3 hours later	Full time NG employee when not at an incident, planning and training	Detection and identification on HAZMAT, assessment, advise and assist with request for additional state and federal resources. Six sections include: C2, communications, admin/logistics, medical/analytical & survey

52,57,80, 81

Table 3 – Key Personnel

Key Personnel	Location	Major Responsibilities related to Public Health (PH) Emergency Management
Defense Coordinating Officers **DCOs**	Ten FEMA Region HQ	-Primary functions is to establish relationships with military, civil and interagency organizations -team consists of 8-12 members
Installation Commander	Base/Post HQ	-Ensure force health measures and PH measures are integrated into response preparedness plans and agreements -Negotiate agreements with local SNS coordinators to serves as resection site and closed POD
Hospital Commander	MTF	-Establish a comprehensive emergency management program integrating PH and medical planning (e.g., mass care, med logistics, MCM acquisition and distribution)
Medical Treatment Facility (MTF) Emergency Manager **MEM**	MTF operation cell	-Coordinate planning and preparedness, and assist in the execution of all-hazards emergency management activities on behalf of the MTF commander
Public Health Emergency Officer **PHEO**	MTF	-Provided Military Commanders with guidance and recommendations on preparing for, declaring, responding to, and recovering from PH emergencies

46,58

Endnotes

[1] Khan S and Richter A. Dispensing Mass Prophylaxis- The Search for the Perfect Solution. *Homeland Security Affairs*, Feb 2012; 8(3).

[2] Risk Management Solutions. Catastrophe, Injury, and Insurance: The impact of Catastrophes on Workman's Compensation, Life and Health Insurance. http://www.rms.com/Publications/Catastrophe_Injury_Insurance.pdf. Accessed February 27, 2012.

[3] Dempsey ME. *Defense Strategy- Sustaining U.S. Global Leadership: Priorities for 21st Century Defense* (Washington, D.C.: U.S. Department of Defense January 2012) 5.

[4] Department of Defense Directive (DoDD) 3025.18. *Defense Support of Civil Authorities (DSCA)*. December 29, 2010.

[5] U. S. Department of Health and Human Services. *National Health Security Strategy of the United States of America.* December 2009. https://www.hsdl.org/?view&did=30691. Accessed January 30, 2012.

[6] The White House. http://www.whitehouse.gov/issues/homeland-security. Accessed January 30, 2012.

[7] Center for Disease Control and Prevention, Emergency Preparedness and Response. Bioterrorism Agents / Diseases. http://emergency.cdc.gov/agent/agentlist-category.asp. Accessed January 14, 2012.

[8] Clark W *Bracing for Armageddon? The Science and Politics of Bioterrorism in America* (New York: Oxford University Press 2008).

[9] Department of Homeland Security and Department of Health and Human Services. *Federal Interagency Concept of Operations- Rapid Medical Countermeasures Dispensing.* September 2011 (Washington, D.C.).

[10] Center for Disease Control and Prevention. Use of Anthrax Vaccine in the United States; Recommendations of the Advisory Committee on Immunization Practices (ACIP), 2009. *MMWR*. July 23,2010; 59(RR-6) 1-36.

[11] Laurie N. Testimony to Committee on Homeland Security and Governmental Affairs U.S. Senate, Safeguarding our Nation: HHS Readiness to Respond to a Biological or Other Emergency. October 18, 2011. http://www.hhs.gov/asl/testify/2011/10/t20111018a.html. Accessed May 27, 2012.

[12] Association of State and Territorial Health Officials. Budget Cuts Continue to Affect the Health of Americans: Update May 2011. ASTHO Research Brief. Arlington, VA, http://www.astho.org/Display/AssetDisplay.aspx?id=6024. Accessed January 28, 2012.

[13] Levi J. Testimony to House Committee on Homeland Security Subcommittee on Emergency Preparedness, Response and Communications. Taking Measure of Countermeasures (Part 2): A Review of Efforets to Protect the Homeland Through Distribution

and Dispensing of CBRN Medical Countermeasures. May 12, 2011.
http://homeland.house.gov/hearing/subcommittee-hearing-taking-measure-countermeasures-part-2-review-efforts-protect-homeland. Accessed March 24, 2012.

[14] Rosner D and Markowitz D *Are We Ready? Public Health since 9/11.* (Burkley: UC Press 2006) 75.

[15] Hodge JG. The Evolution of Law in Biopreparedness. *Biosecurity and Bioterrorism: Biodefense Strategy. Practice, and Science. 2012;* 10(1) doi: 10.1089/bsp.2011.0094.

[16] Center for Disease Control and Prevention, CDC Cities Readiness Initiative. http://www.bt.cdc.gov/cri. Accessed September 16, 2011.

[17] Nelson C. Federal Initiative Increases Community Preparedness for Public Health Emergencies. *Health Affairs,* 2010; 29(12) : 2286.

[18] Pandemic and All-Hazards Preparedness Act. PUBLIC LAW 109–417—DEC. 19, 2006, 109th Congress.

[19] Saure, LM, MCCarthy, ML, Knabel, A, Brewster, P. Concepts in Disaster Medicine: Major Influences on Hospital Emergency Management and Disaster Preparedness. *Disaster Medicine and Public Health Preparedness.* June 1, 2009. http://www.dmphp.org/cgi/content/full/3/Supplement_1/S68. Accessed March 23, 2012.

[20] Obama B. Executive Order 13527. Establishing Federal Capability for the Timely Provision of Medical Countermeasures Following a Biological Attack. December 30, 2009.

[21] Johnstone, RW *Bioterror: Anthrax, Influenza, and the Future of Public Health Security* (Westport, CN: Praeger Security International 2008) 126.

[22] National Association of County & City Health Officials. Local Health Department Job Losses and Program Cuts: Findings from January 2012 Survey. March 2012. http://www.naccho.org/topics/infrastructure/lhdbudget/upload/Overview-Report-Final-2.pdf. Accessed April 4, 2012.

[23]Trust for America's Health, *Ready or Not? Protecting the Public's Health from Disease, Disasters, and Bioterrorism 2011 Issue Report.* December 2011. http://www.healthyamericans.org/assets/files/TFAH2011ReadyorNot_09.pdf. Accessed January 4, 2012.

[24] Senate Passes PAHPA. Reauthorization of Biodefense Programs with some variations from House. *GEN News Highlights:* March 12, 20112.*GEN Genetic Engineering & Biotechnology News.* http://www.genengnews.com/keywordsandtools/print/4/26363/. Accessed March 25, 2012.

[25] U.S. Department of Homeland Security. *National Preparedness Guidelines.* September 2007. 31.

[26] Gursky EA and Bice G. Assessing a Decade of Public Health Preparedness: Progress on the Precipice? *Biosecurity and Bioterrorism: Biodefense Strategy. Practice, and Science.2012;* 10(1) doi: 10.1089/bsp.2011.0085.

[27] Institute of Medicine of the National Academies, *Prepositioning Antibiotics for Anthrax: A Decision-Aiding Framework.* (Washington, D.C., The National Academies Press 2012). 15.5.

[28] National Association of County and City Health Officials, *2010 National Profile of Local Health Departments.* Aug 2011. http://www.naccho.org/topics/infrastructure/profile/resources/2010report/upload/2010_Profile_main_report-web.pdf. Accessed March 21, 2012.

[29] Gursky E, Inglesby T, and O'Toole T. Anthrax 2001: Observations on the Medical and Public Health Response. B*iosecurity and Bioterrorism: Biodefense Strategy, Practice and Science.* Nov 2, 2003; 1(2):107.

[30] Flynn S, *The Edge of Disaster: Rebuilding a Resilient Nation* (New York, Random House, 2007). 75.

[31] Weapons of Mass Destruction Center, *Bipartisan WMD Terrorism Research Center's Bio-Response Report Card.* (Washington, D.C. Oct 2011). 8.

[32] Department of Homeland Security. *National Preparedness Goal – First Edition.* September 2011, http://www.fema.gov/pdf/prepared/npg.pdf. Accessed February 2, 2012.

[33] Tussing BB. Implementing a New Vision: Unity of Effort in Preparing for and Responding to Catastrophic Events. Center for Strategic Leadership Issue Paper, U.S. Army War College March 2011;I 2(11) CSL-4.

[34] Orderno RT. 2011 AUSA Eisenhower Luncheon remarks October 11, 2011. http://www.army.mil.article/67090/. Accessed January 12, 2012.

[35] Jones JM. Americans Most Confident in Military, Least in Congress. June 23, 2011 http://www.gallup.com/poll/148163/americans-confident-military-least-congress.aspx?version=print. Accessed March 26, 2012.

[36] Gates RE. *Quadrennial Defense Review* (Washington, D.C.: U.S. Department of Defense, February 2010). 19.

[37] Seattle participant comments, Medical Countermeasure Public Engagement Initiative. November 4-5, 2011. Hosted by Department of Medical Countermeasures Strategy and Response, Office of the Assistant Secretary for Preparedness and Response, Department of Health and Human Services.

[38] Ingram, WE, Security America Can Afford; Army National Guard Posture Statement. http://www.nationalguard.mil/features/ngps/web/index.html. Accessed March 20, 2012.

[39] Government Accounting Office, *Catastrophic Disasters: Enhanced Leadership, Capabilities, and Accountability Controls Will Improve the Effectiveness of the Nation's*

Preparedness, Response, and Recovery System, GAO- 06-618. Washington D.C. September 2006.

[40] Government Accounting Office, *Better Plans and Exercises Needed to Guide the Military's Response to Catastrophic Natural Disasters*, GAO-06-643. Washington D.C.; May 2006.

[41] Advisory Panel on DoD Capabilities for Support of Civil Authorities After Certain incidents, *Before Disaster Strikes: Imperatives for Enhancing Defense Support of Civil Authorities.* September 15. 2010.

[42] United Stated Northern Command. http://www.northcom.mil/. Accessed March 21, 2012.

[43] Winnefeld JA. Commander's Estimate – USNORTHCOM Support to Medical Countermeasures Distribution and Dispensing, Peterson AFB, Colorado, May 17, 2011.

[44] Department of Defense Instruction (DoDI) 6200.03 *Public Health Emergency Management Within the Department of Defense.* March 2010.

[45] Morris JC, Morris ED, Jones DM. Reaching for the Philosopher's Stone: Contingent Coordination and the Military's response to Hurricane Katrina. *Public Administration Review.* December 2007; Special Issue, 98.

[46] McHew JM and Ordierno RT. *2012 Army Posture Statement: The Nation's Force of Decisive Action.* (Washington, DC: U.S. Department of the Army, 2012) Information paper Defense Coordinating Officer (DCO) Defense Coordinating Element (DCE) Agency: US Army North (USARNORTH) posted on Mon, 2012-02-06, https://secureweb2.hqda.pentagon.mil/VDAS_ArmyPostureStatement/2012/. Accessed February 22, 2012.

[47] U.S. Army War College. *How the Army Runs: A Senior Leader's Reference Handbook*, 28th ed Harold W. Lord (editor) Chapter 22- Defense Support to Civil Authorities. 2012.

[48] Chairman of the Joint Chiefs of Staff Instruction 3125.01B. *Defense Support of Civil Authorities (CSCA) for Domestic Consequence Management (CM) Operations in Response to a Chemical, Biological, Radiological, Nuclear, or High-Yield Explosive (CBRNE) Incident.* August 19, 2009.

[49] Army North PAO and National Guard Bureau, Key Leaders meet at domestic preparedness workshop to discuss providing civil support. February 29, 2012. http://www.army.mil/article/74690/Key_leaders_meet_at_domestic_preparedness_workshop_to_discuss_providing_civil_support/.. Accessed March 7, 2012.

[50] U.S. Army War College. *How the Army Runs: A Senior Leader's Reference Handbook*, 28th ed Harold W. Lord (editor) Chapter 22. Defense Support to Civil Authorities. 2012.

[51] Joint Task Force Civil Support. http://www.jtfcs.northcom.mil/JTFCS.aspx. Accessed March 21, 2012.

[52] Stewart X and Oberholtzer W. The Continuity Gap. *CST & CBRNE Source Book.* June 2011: 10.

[53] Greenhill J Hundreds of National Guard troops responding to Midwestern, Southern tornados. March 3, 2012. US. Army. http://www.army.mil/article/74988/ . Accessed March 20, 2012.

[54] Insurance Claims from Recent Tornadoes May Top $1B. *Insurance Journal.* http://www.insurancejournal.com/news/midwest/2012/03/05/238355.htm. Accessed March 20, 2012.

[55] DanielM. *EarthSky News.* March 5, 2012. http://earthsky.org/earth/recap-of-deadly-u-s-tornado-outbreak-february-28-march-3-2012. Accessed March 20, 2012.

[56] Ingram, WE, *Security America Can Afford; Army National Guard Posture Statement,* http://www.nationalguard.mil/features/ngps/web/index.html. Accessed March 20, 2012.

[57] National Guard Public Affairs. Bulking Up First Response Capabilities. *CST & CBRNE,* June 2011, 33.

[58] LeJeune C. Consequence Management: Steps in the Right Direction? *National Security Watch,* September 2, 2010;10(2) 4.

[59] Mc Hew JM and Ordierno RT. *2012 Army Posture Statement: The Nation's Force of Decisive Action.* (Washington, DC: U.S. Department of the Army, 2012) Information paper National Guard Weapons of Mass Destruction Civil Support Teams Agency: Army National Guard (ARNG) posted 2012-02-06, https://secureweb2.hqda.pentagon.mil/VDAS_ArmyPostureStatement/2012/. Accessed February 22, 2012.

[60] Waugh WL. EMAC, Katrina, and the Governors of Louisiana and Mississippi. *Public Administration Review,* December 2007, Special Issue, 107.

[61] Joint Commission for Accreditation of Hospital Organizations. http://www.jointcommission.org/. Accessed March 5, 2012.

[62] Saure LM, MCCarthy ML, Knabel A, Brewster P. Concepts in Disaster Medicine: Major Influences on Hospital Emergency Management and Disaster Preparedness. *Disaster Medicine and Public Health Preparedness.* June 1, 2009 http://www.dmphp.org/cgi/content/full/3/Supplement_1/S68. Accessed March 23, 2012.

[63] Horaho PA. The Surgeon General of the United States Army with testimony for Committee on Appropriations Subcommittee on Defense, U.S. House of Representatives, 2nd sec, 112th Congress. FY 2013 Defense Health Program Hearing. March 8, 2012.

[64] Personal communication, LTC Cory N. Costello, Division Surgeon, 1st Cavalry Division, Fort Hood, TX. December 2011.

[65] Advisory Panel on Department of Defense Capabilities for Support of Civil Authorities After Certain Incidents, "Before Disaster Strikes: Imperatives for Enhancing Defense Support of Civil Authorities," September 15, 2010.

[66] Wagner G. Navy, Local Officials Agree to Regional Community Relations Council. Naval Support Activity South Potomac . http://www.cnic.navy.mil/SPotomac/NewsAndCurrentInfo/PressReleases/CNICC_053258. Accessed March 9, 2012.

[67] Revelos A. COMREL Council brings local leaders together. *dcmilitary.com*. online magazine http://ww2.dcmilitary.com/stories/051911/southpotomac_28283.shtml . Accessed March 9, 2012.

[68] Lesperance AM et. Ala Developing a Regional Recovery Framework. *Biosecurity and Bioterrorism: Biodefense Strategy, Practice, and Science.* 2001;9(3) 280-287.

[69] Mackenzie C et. al. How Will Military/Civilian Coordination Work for Reception of Mass Casualties from Overseas? *Prehospital Disaster Medicine*, September –October 2009; 24(5) http://pdm.medicine.wisc.edu. web publication. Accessed January 25, 2012.

[70] University of Minnesota. Preparedness Activities Inform a Coordinated Response to Fort Hood Shooting (TX). Public Health practices: Enhancing Emergency Preparedness and Response. http://www.publichealthpractices.org/practice/preparedness-activities-inform-coordinated-response-fort-hood-shooting-tx. Accessed April 11, 2012.

[71] KWTX.COM. Sunday is 20th Anniversary of Killen Luby's Cafeteria Massacre. October 16, 2011. http://www.kwtx.com/localnews/headlines/Sunday_Is_20th_Anniversary_Of_Killeen_Lubys_Cafeteria_Massacre_131944868.html. Accessed March 9, 2012.

[72] Morris JC, Morris ED, and Jones DM. Reaching the Philosophers' Stone: Contingent Coordination and the Military's Response to Hurricane Katrina. *Public Administration Review.* December 2007, Special Issue,103.

[73] Huber GA, Cambell DR, Dorman K, and McIntosh L. Joint Readiness Center- Pittsburgh: A Model of Military- Civilian Readiness And Response. *Commonwealth: A Journal of Political Science.* May 2009;15 Policy on Emergency Management.

[74] Anderson K.. Army North leads way during large-scale terrorism response exercise. www.army.mil. August 13, 2011. http://www.army.mil/article/64080/Army_North_leads_way_during_large_scale_terrorism_response_exercise Accessed October 13, 2011.

[75] Manuszewski D. Army North gears up for Vibrant Response 11.1. United States Northern Command. March 10, 2011 http://www.northcom.mil/news/2011/031011.html Accessed October 13, 2011

[76] Cannon E. Vibrant Response 12' Mass Catastrophe Exercise Takes Place in the Heartland. *Chicago Homeland Security Examiner.* Aug, 23, 2011

http://www.examiner.com/homeland-security-in-chicago/vibrant-response-12-mass-catastrophe-excercise-takes-place-the-heartland#ixzz1VwGzVOBd. Accessed January 17, 2012.

[77] *Homeland Security News Wire*, Operation Vigilant Guard tests Arizona disaster Response, NOV 11,2011. http://www.nationalguard.mil/news/archives/2011/11/110711-Vigilant.aspne:. Accessed January 20, 2012.

[78] Department of Homeland Security, *Homeland Security Exercise and Evaluation Program (HSEEP)* Volume III; Exercise Evaluation and Improvement Planning, February 2007.

[79] U.S. Army North. http://www.arnorth.army.mil/About-ARNORTH.aspx. Accessed March 2, 2012.

[80] Mc Hew JM and Ordierno RT. *2012 Army Posture Statement: The Nation's Force of Decisive Action.* (Washington, DC: U.S. Department of the Army, 2012) https://secureweb2.hqda.pentagon.mil/VDAS_ArmyPostureStatement/2012/. Accessed February 22, 2012.

[81] Mc Hew JM and Ordierno RT. *2012 Army Posture Statement: The Nation's Force of Decisive Action* (Washington, DC: U.S. Department of the Army, 2012) Information paper : "Chemical, Biological, Radiological and Nuclear (CBRN) Response Enterprise Agency: US Army North" (USARNORTH) posted 2012-02-06, https://secureweb2.hqda.pentagon.mil/VDAS_ArmyPostureStatement/2012/. Accessed February 22, 2012.

www.ingramcontent.com/pod-product-compliance
Lightning Source LLC
Chambersburg PA
CBHW081808280526
45789CB00008B/3051